A LITTLE BOOK OF INSPIRATION

A LITTLE BOOK OF INSPIRATION

By James O'Sullivan *et al*

First published in 2013 by Thynks Publications Limited.

Registered Office:
White House, Clarendon Street, Nottingham, NG1 5GF England

http://www.thynkspublications.co.uk

Copyright © James O'Sullivan *et al*, 2013

Each poet, whose work is included in this book,
owns the copyright to the poems associated with their name:

Arthur Carr, Bruno Alexandre Gomes Rodrigues, Claire Cox,
Desmond Kon, Don Nixon, Dorrie Pearton, George Reith,
Gwendoline Hartland, James Nuthall, James O'Sullivan, Jean Cardy,
Judith Tremayne Drazin, June Drake, Luke Jackson, Margaret Pedley,
Mark Mikklesen, Meirion Tanner, Michael Borlase, Nick Boreham,
Panayiotis Vyras, Patricia Sumner, Richard Gills,
Susan Thompson.

All rights reserved

Typesetting and Printing by
Book Printing UK
Remus House
Coltsfoot Drive
Woodston
Peterborough PE2 9BF.

ISBN: 978-1-900410-60-1

CONTENTS

CONTENTS	i
PUBLISHER'S FOREWORD	v
Arthur Carr	**1**
A Smile at the Window	1
Bruno Alexandre Gomes Rodrigues	**2**
Untitled	2
Claire Cox	**3**
White Buffalo's Gift	3
Desmond Kon	**4**
If Jeffrey Smart Painted James Joyce	4
Little Girl's Antistrophe	6
Don Nixon	**9**
Dietrich Bonhoeffer – An Inspiration	9
Dorrie Pearton	**10**
Hunter Gatherer	10
George Reith	**12**
Swan Song	12

Gwendoline Hartland	14
The Spitfire and its Pilots	14
James Nuthall	15
We're in this Together	15
James O'Sullivan	17
Gougane Barra	17
Jean Cardy	18
London Changes	18
Sound Waves	19
Judith Tremaine Drazin	20
The Ancient Orchard	20
The Dowser	21
June Drake	22
An Amputee	22
Our Gran	24
Luke Jackson	26
Fleeting Thoughts	26
Margaret Pedley	27
Awakening	27

Mark Mikkelsen	**29**
Ex Tempore VII	29
Meirion Tanner	**31**
To My Children	31
Michael Borlase	**32**
Mother/Teacher	32
Nick Boreham	**33**
Antler	33
Early Easter	34
Going Back	35
Igloos	37
Panayiotis Vyras	**39**
Angels	39
Patricia Sumner	**40**
Early Morning, Cilan	40
Symphony	41
Moment	43
Richard Gills	**44**
Spring	44

Susan Thompson **46**

    Who's With Me?   46

PUBLISHERS FOREWORD

This book sprang from the results of a poetry competition on the theme of Inspiration.

The top three prizewinners were:

1. *Gougane Barra by James O'Sullivan
2. The Dowser by Judith Tremayne Drazin
3. Little Girl's Antistrophe by Desmond Kon

Gougane Barra brings something of the magic of Ireland to the reader. Here, tucked away in County Cork, it is said that St. Finbarr built a monastery at some stage in the 6th century.

James O'Sullivan says: *There is peace there for all who seek freedom from the burden of man, or any such creature that breathes.*

There are many other delightfully inspiring poems in this collection.

ARTHUR CARR

A SMILE AT THE WINDOW

There are some dear souls who live alone
In the peace of their self-content
There are souls apart, who no-one knows
With kindness of heart heaven-sent

There are pioneer souls making their way
Over roads they've never run
But let me sit by my window
And give my help to any man

Just give me the chance to help if I can
Where the tide of life passes by
Some men are open and some men are shy
Much the same as you or I

From the men who are able and try
To those who are beaten down low
I'll not choose to sit as a judge
And scorn their lifetime plan

Life has narrow lanes and highways ahead
With mountains of challenging height
The days are long and there are challenges
That may continue well into the night

But I am happy for those who celebrate
And offer solace to those who cry
So let me sit in my seat at the window
And offer help to all who may pass by

BRUNO ALEXANDRE GOMES RODRIGUES

UNTITLED

We were in the icy wastes of Antarctica
the crystalline lake of *memory*
and in those lonely days the world was nothing and the number we
made gleamed brightly
like a star
a quasar
pulsing energy through *space*
and through *time*.

Memories & dreams dancing together.
The love of the past tense in future time.
Never in the present.
The memories of dreams and memories in dreams.

A place of re-encounter as a childhood island on adult time:
a place where we belong.
The silence.
What we are.

The stage where the soul can dance at her own pleasure.

CLAIRE COX

WHITE BUFFALO'S GIFT

And flesh flew away
and it is winter and the flat
frost-stiff land breathes
under the lengthening night.

Moon-shadow wolves ghost-silent
by the lake. In the hearth,
a lamp, a shaving from
summer's sun, light for

evening chores, the shared
breath, the heart's glimmer.
And each heart is a small blaze:
a scattered beacon far across

the wilderness, but
spaceless in the One Heart,
the One Summer, winter's
indivisible twin.

DESMOND KON

IF JEFFREY SMART PAINTED JAMES JOYCE

> I must have looked like a fellow throwing a handful of peas into the air.
> People began to look at us. She shook hands a moment after
> and, in going away, said she hoped I would do what I said.
>
> ~ James Joyce

It would have been in Rathgar, outside a steel mill.

The building seated in its shadow, top row of windows
now shattered glass – a boy facing east, hurling balls of coal.
There was an ice climber's cord hanging from his outpost,
knotted with caster wheels. It looked like a rope ladder.

Smart used a disegno, measured every angle, each inch
of scaffolding another space for a softer bit of street yellow.

The brick orange was added for Joyce's cheekbones.

I saw Keats returning from the rose garden with a sonnet.
The garden belonged to an old miner, its bushes brittle and dry.
It looked strange, a small cottage surrounded by a picket fence,
and beside it, a landfill that ran a mile into Naul Hills.

Yet free of it. Keats had fallen asleep, the way Severn sketched him.
Fanny Brawne in relief, standing a few yards from him.
Near another window, a barn swallow eating from her hand.

The painting looked like a pastoral. Idyllic. Distant.
Crepe roses behind Joyce. Stadium lights. The freeway of no cars.

Living in the city is deafening. London teaches you
to ignore the immediate moment, the overturned crate in the alley.
Bags of beans split open. Sprawling lentils. Lima beans, pinto beans.

Your eyes turn lazy, the stoplight to tell you when to stall or go.

The bin to throw your brown bag into. London forcing you
to locate particularity – things, relevance, connection, longing as love.
Something to be done. The route to the library where you'll sit
in the far right corner, on the big chair riveted to the ground.

It was closing time at the mill, black mask of figures in contrapposto.

The disegno looked like an origami pattern for a rose,
its mosaic tiling of mountain folds, ridge folds and valley folds.

The boy took it in his hand, placed the coal neatly within it.
Wrapping it in, he handed it to Smart and asked for a drawing.

---

* This poem was written on 13 January 2011, to mark the 70th death anniversary of James Joyce. The epigraph is an excerpt from *Portrait of the Artist*. Jeffrey Smart is one of Australia's most renowned painters, now residing in Tuscany.

DESMOND KON

LITTLE GIRL'S ANTISTROPHE AT 27 RUE DE FLEURES

Just now, I unwrapped her box of letters. Gertrude was an iconoclast
to her gravitas. What she did not know she let travel, recurrence
of rhymes like falling leaves buffeting, autumn breeze from East Side.
Gertrude did not know home tonight or home in the summer.
By the Hudson. Did not know pudding from sauce from Helfgott's letters.

Its mention of parlor poetry as dried hydrangea as pastoral,
as another Gothic point of view. As the bird feeder broke into two,
as freer roads after the scuttling, as prying apart the living architectonics.
Like her piano rolled down the stairs. Of play and vinaigrette
and too much cayenne. That the Tribune was the Tribune after all.

But also a need and problem within the chronic hours.
Gertrude did not know the object beyond the object.
Beyond the waterfowl, a duck of oval, of beak and weathervane wing,
of zipper heart, and an accordion tongue. Gertrude did not know
where to put the centre of things. Gertrude did not soak Henry's cloak.

Nor Mildred's, its hem another herringbone stitch, another section
not whole enough or wholehearted or wholemeal enough.
The whole world was no longer a lazy afternoon or abiding love,
an old Gertrude looking at herself in the mirror of the ponding water.
Her head taking the shape of the barn, its shadow a black soot.

In midday sun, quiet afternoon cradling itself into the moonless night.
Gertrude was earnest in losing things – the beat-up rosebush
one more variation, foot divisions misaligned, word endings falling
over each other, frothy tumble. Gertrude's diaeresis, Alice in a deep sleep,
the lean and fallow years from that trembling point onwards.

Gertrude's dactylic dimeter drumming itself into the hexameter,
a twist as with the helix, as with rollercoaster feelings
when affectations run wild, when The Salon levitated
into *The Cloud of Unknowing*, its noetic white as wispy and dissolving.
Then a removal so she would always ask more questions.

As supple as her very last. Gertrude's Sunday clatter in another suite
to rile Chaucer, even in death, even in love from a distance.
Even in wise restraint and a portrait left in the dark, its phonic echoes
a new refrain of face and facet. And fractured verseforms.
Gertrude's sudden awakening to sovereignity's shining eye.

Not decadence but wonderment. Not meaninglessness but a prayer,
a detachment and reasoned feeling. A small run of sounds and pictures.
Of a sapling writing out its unknown destination, its basis
and other evidence scaffolding, relaxed into a vine far down the road.
In the vineyard, a redder rose held out in the palm of her hand.

DON NIXON

DIETRICH BONHOEFFER – AN INSPIRATION

His portrait shows an ordinary face,
Pleasant but unremarkable, the type
You see in any German market-place –
A prosperous Saxon burgher stereotype.
But look again. You see it in the eyes
And in the firm set of the mouth and chin,
This pastor who defied the Third Reich's lies,
While knowing there was no way he could win.
Condemned and tortured, bravely he spoke out.
Only his strong faith was left to sustain
Him. Decades on, his voice still calls, a shout
For man's conscience, the noose cannot restrain.
He still inspires us through his sacrifice,
Reminding us our freedom has a price.

DORRIE PEARTON

HUNTER GATHERER

To make a harvest supper
as the summer ends
visit the flowing stream.
Gather lush watercress
washed in the fastest flow.
Simmer slowly for soup.

Put your crayfish basket
at the nearby bend
but hope you'll
meet a friend on the bridge
who has caught too many
and shares his bounty with you.

Spice your thanks with laughter,
entice him back to supper.
Hunt for mushrooms,
their parasols first day fresh.
Gently sauté until the aroma fills the air.

Wander through the meadow
to where the rocket grows,
and find the wild mint.
With them make your salad.
Add hazlenuts, perfect,
as you take them from their bonnets.

Collect shining blackberries
in your sky-blue bowl.
(Gently remove the small stripy snail.)
Brim to the top with red ripe bullaces.
Savour the juice on your fingers
as whispers of flavours ahead.
Sip an infusion of
summer honey heather flowers,
toast each other's health.
Cook outside. Count with wonder
the shooting stars
and the richness of your supper.

GEORGE REITH

SWAN SONG

It was on a Wednesday my travels, abrupt,

were stopped by a sight that wrestled a gaze.

In all the times of all my days

Ne'er could the sight of a bird interrupt.

A swan careened in the pier on a bay

So far from the gardens of royal domain

Faced with this rarity, what can I say

to recount her presence so her image may remain?

That silent eloper who, sole, betrays

the mute of the scene, barren and grey.

With sepulchral dress, my love in disguise

murks through the water to catch my eyes.

Those efforts concealed, her bill glares on,

judging the stalks I was walking upon.

How could I hide the things that I am,

The flesh and bones that makes a man a man?

I ask these questions not out of indecision,

for what man wouldn't falter in my position?

With all her grace, how could I atone

and do any more than limp my way home?

GWENDOLINE HARTLAND

THE SPITFIRE AND ITS PILOTS

On Remembrance Sunday in November
A Spitfire flies over the memorial
Gathering at the Cenotaph, over
The Mall, and Buckingham Palace

The unmistakable sound of the engine
Stirs memories in the minds of survivors,
Both defenders and defended, who lived
Through the Second World War

They live again the exciting
Terrible days of "The Few" when
Those hard-winged wasps dived
And spun, and stung our enemies.

The future will always see hands
Raised to shade against
The welcome sun, anxious not to lose
Sight of the Merlin magic, remembering

The men who bought time
With Mitchell's metal steeds
Together they saved this island
Their fortitude and youthful
Sacrifice noted in our history
For ever. Never to be forgotten.

JAMES NUTHALL

WE'RE IN THIS TOGETHER

Our lives are not like North Korea,
Whose people starve and die in fear.
But repression comes in many forms;
Our money lost within the laws.

The working people shrug and moan,
While banks will gamble what we own.
We watch the richest dodging tax
As public servants get the axe.

They speak to you in practised smile;
They give an inch and take a mile.
We pay for more, and get back less,
To stuff the mouths of one percent.

What will they do to make us fight,
And question what we need in life?

So avoid-a-phone, topple the shop;
Let's raise the low, bring down the top.
Don't shrug, don't moan then pay the cost
To replace the money that they all lost.

We'll rock the boat, our sinking ship,
And fill the holes they put in it.
Now make a noise and huddle in;
We'll counteract their PR spin.

Let's raise our arms, they've not yet won;
Make the greedy know what can be done.
Move forward now in peaceful fight;
Show them the path we know is right.

JAMES O'SULLIVAN

GOUGANE BARRA

Beneath the Silver Mountains it lies –
that tapestry of green, deep in the hollow,
along the fabled banks where stoics slept.
Her ancient mouth hangs open still –
countless lines were built upon her words,
as down through the ages they crept.
Those forgotten words do not speak
of time, but of secrets, passed among birds
who have been bred upon those branches.
There is peace there for all who seek
freedom from the burden of man,
or any such creature that breathes.

Here, among the branches, lie the gates
of Arcadia, covered by dark moss.
Deep in the stillness, that utopia waits
for those who would boldly cross
its threshold, taking from the Fates
that which has been our greatest loss.

Beneath the Silver Mountains it lies –
that tapestry of green, deep in the hollow,
where stoics slept and visions walk freely
without fear of life's endless ties.

JEAN CARDY

LONDON CHANGES

So it was a lovely day,
late Autumn,
a last farewell to Summer,
warm enough to lunch out
in a courtyard,
with wasps.
We would, in the past,
have flocked to the countryside:
Epping Forest, the sea.
Today we celebrate the sun
in London;
a procession of river-boats,
packed tight, a sea of heads;
strollers thick along the South Bank,
busy tables outside each pub or café,
sunglasses everywhere.
London has changed, relaxed.

JEAN CARDY

SOUND WAVES

Somewhere out in the dark reaches
of the universe
sound waves endlessly flow.
Suppose that one day
future scientists
can capture those waves,
recall them,
tentatively at first,
like early wireless,
then with more and more certainty.
Imagine hearing Keats
reading his odes,
Chaucer, the Beowulf poet,
Shakespeare the actor.
Many poets sound odd,
reading their own work:
think T.S. Eliot,
think Tennyson.
There would be shocks.
And the language would have changed;
it would need study
to hear those voices,
but imagine it;
to be able to dial up
Socrates, Dante, Plato.

JUDITH TREMAYNE DRAZIN

THE ANCIENT ORCHARD

Late morning and prepared to go

Towards the white twisting road

The treacherous road, took us instead

Towards the ancient orchard where

The light is green and apples grow

Such teasing apples, bittersweet

The children turning feral, swing

From mossy branches. Bright the air

Of Indian Summer. Rich the scent

Of mould and change and ferny earth.

Shedding your city ways you made

A wreath of daisies for my hair.

JUDITH TREMAYNE DRAZIN

THE DOWSER

At family picnics when
The thin blue woodsmoke curled
From makeshift campfires and
As gathering starlings, Aunts
And zealous Mothers swirled
Dispensing food and chat
While children tumbled like
Bright beads in drifts of grass
Alone, apart, he sat.

'He's not exactly' said
My Auntie June 'Be kind'
He liked collecting things
Acorns and mossy stones
Whatever he could find
Forked twigs of hazel, may
The time he tried to woo
Us with his silly gifts
We laughed and turned away.

Late Summer, buzzing flies
Dry grass, tired hedgerows, blight
Where once clear streamlets flowed
Now mud and shifting sand
Stretched onwards out of sight
Cross children whined but he
Stood tall and held his wand
Of hazel over bare
Dead earth. Springing it came
The lovely water, bright
Entranced, we turned to stare.

JUNE DRAKE

AN AMPUTEE

My neighbour nods, a greeting of a sort,
but never yells a cheery, loud "hello".
Perhaps he fears I'd hear it as gun shots,
behave like some demented soldier, thinks
it best to take the cotton-wool approach.
He doesn't know, was never sent abroad
with lots of other healthy, fighting friends
who came back either incomplete or dead.
He can't afford to let his mind conceive
a situation where he's lamed like me:
he lacks the courage to make that a fact.

I won't hide out of sight to spare his blush,
conceal myself: a man who lacks a leg,
who's had to learn to stand and walk afresh,
pretend he doesn't care he cannot run
or kick a football with the local lads.
Yes, pride took injury by its fleshy scruff
and twisted it 'til military erect
to spare embarrassment of such as he,
my neighbour, faking silent sympathy
in his brief nod across the garden wall
because he cannot share in what I've seen.

I'm neither bitter nor make space for praise
and will not dive into depression's grip;
spare me the turned-down lip, the deep-set frown
that makes an ugly gargoyle of a face.
Not many service-men fall in that trap,
they just want plain acceptance of the fact
they are disabled now, not wrapped in shawls
but on display as what they are, maintain
life-styles well adapted to their needs,
unlabelled too. My neighbour doesn't know
how I would like a friendly-voiced "hello".

JUNE DRAKE

OUR GRAN

Of course, I never knew her as a girl
but can believe how Grandma brightly shone
to bait the boys, like lustre of a pearl.

She chose to wed one handsome, stylish John
not long before the 14/18 war.
'Your country needs you!' echoed. John was gone!

The child growing in Gran's womb she bore
with mingled joy and fear: she was naive.
The girl was born and placed within a drawer

as was the custom. John came home on leave,
was thrilled to see the babe – though not a lad.
This time it was twin boys she would conceive.

The state in which the men returned was bad,
some shell-shocked, others just about alive,
not wounded. But T.B. was what John had

and he would die. By then young Grace was five
and Grandma poor, but day and night she slaved
so that her little ones could eat and thrive.

Resolve and self-respect were never waived
and as the children grew they did their share
of work. What's more, each one was well-behaved.

It's said, 'a family without a man
is lacking solid roots'. Not Gran's. Indeed,
there's none I've ever known that can compare.

Grandchildren and their friends alike, would feed
from her continual love: she was our Creed.

LUKE JACKSON

FLEETING THOUGHTS

I have black and white feathers tattooed on my chest,
My guardian angel's wings sprawled across my breast,
It seems with these wings I cannot fly,
As I wish, way up high into the blue, blue sky.
Fly away, soar, that's all I want to do,
Glide amongst the clouds, take in the view.
Looking out the window I see birds weaving through the trees,
I'll dive out this window, join them and we'll tease
Everybody and everything not gifted with heavenly flight,
Men will look and long, just able to bear such a sight.
The pride I have in my wonderful ink wings,
I feel like I can fly just thinking of the things,
The power of thought, the power of suggestion,
Amazing what you can achieve with a little direction,
Whatever you want, whatever you believe,
Anything you can think of, you can conceive.
Ambition, motivation, that's all that you need,
Create an idea, in your mind plant a seed,
Think outside the box, that's what they all say,
I say step outside the box and let us play
With thoughts, with ideas, we'll even play with the world,
The world is my playground, the Earth is my pearl,
For I am Alpha, Omega, I am the Almighty,
I am what I am, and all that I might be.

MARGARET PEDLEY

AWAKENING

Hope is forever immortalised in

the first birdsong at dawn

as others join in, one solitary song

becomes a chorus of joy.

As the sun rises higher

so too do our dreams.

From such a perfect beginning

must come a glorious end

the part in-between – held in our hands

will be created with love,

Setting sail with a focus

pitching and tossing on

the sea of our desires;

we gaze at distant shores

journeying on and forever on

searching for more

we must be certain, always sure.

Where is the place that holds our heart?

In front or behind?

Perhaps where we stand.

MARK MIKKLESEN

EX TEMPORE VII
For G.

For the music I cannot draw
For the pictures I cannot write
For the sounds I wish I saw
There are those that I might

For the places of which I dream
For the tastes I hope to breathe
For the things I really mean
May rhyme and reason never leave

For the love I long ago lost
For that which did not come
For the paths that did not cross
There is still little and some

For the goals still unreached
For the struggles not yet won
For the walls that sometimes breach
Tomorrow will see a new sun

For the many occasions I reminisce
For what are now but memories
For all the days that I miss
There is still much for me to see

For age that creeps and creeps
For the time that slips away
For mountains now too steep
There will be stories to recount and lay

For the mistakes that I made
For the regret that burns
For the words I mislaid
I can and will always learn

For the fear that restrains
For when around me there are none
For the times ruled by pain
It is I who will overcome

For all this and more
For what will come and what came before
There is me, there is you
And this is all we ever need know

MEIRION TANNER

TO MY CHILDREN

I will be the barrier upon which the waves of our history will crash

I will be the guard at the gate

I will hold you while you rage against the world that will not do your bidding

And I will stand for you when you cannot or will not stand for yourself.

You will play amidst my shelter, innocent and unknowing

And you will feel the strength of my love as you enter the world,

Openhearted, passionate and free.

MICHAEL BORLASE

MOTHER/TEACHER

So this is what it must be like to be dreaming real dreams
No more name tags being sewn into the seams
of clothes we bought for school.
Where on first days I'd be caught hiding
telling teachers that I wanted you.

But come the end of day
my bag is flapping as I run to greet you by the gates.
Then walking home and holding hands.
Me impatient just to play.

The sunset means it's only getting colder
Knowing only sadness
That we're never going to hold her
again and again we reach out, lips pursed
but in these last few months the news has been only getting worse.

Golden and bright like the last phoenix burning
She has been the teacher of life's lessons worth learning
And so in this dream unreal
A tragedy we cannot fight
I dedicate this to my Mother
Who taught me how to read and write.

NICK BOREHAM

ANTLER

In the quiet of the forest,

on a bed of leaves beside a stream

I found an antler,

perfect, newly shed, warm to the touch.

An intricate wonder, a marvel I could imagine

crashing through bracken in moonlight

under a sky my breath would catch on.

And the deer who had left it on that dark hill

sharing the moment with me,

motionless among the trees.

I knelt there breathless, knowing

that there were two of us listening to the wind;

two of us

listening to the water

trickling across the rocks.

NICK BOREHAM

EARLY EASTER

You left the patio door open for a while
so that I could see the buds
gather strength from their sweet stalks
and the sun come across the threshold
to escape the March wind.
How the church bells crashed
that early Easter!
And in their bright moment showed me
blood. Nails.
Death in resurrection spanning the sky,
carrying away my dark thoughts
like dry stalks blown out to sea by the wind
over the headland over the lighthouse
over the white flecks of the waves
scattered
purified
gone

NICK BOREHAM

GOING BACK

It's where I grew up. The valley,

dandelion-yellow in June.

The caves. The abandoned mine,

still flooded by winter snow.

The ancient drover's trail visible from the top of the crags.

Below me, the limestone cliffs quiver with nesting birds,

while on a nearby hill, bales of new-mown hay

point their shadows to where an overloaded bale-trolley

squeals out a cry for help, stuck on a slope.

Swallows dive-bomb the cottage in which we used to live

the way they did each summer,

remembering the nests they built the previous year.

Less intelligent than they,

my own remembering calls back

farms, neighbours, animals. Us.

Shadows feeding off the warmth of the grass

under dry stone walls.

Trees along the tops of the ridges,

their branches roaring in the wind.

A dog barking in the next valley.

Fifteen years is a long time.

Where I live now, city streets cough into each others' mouths

and citizens compress their anonymities

into meagre spaces, sparsely existing.

But here's another world.

Curlews have built a nest

in the hollow in front of our cottage,

smoke from distant farms drifts through the walled wood

where hunters flatten the velvet bracken

and I am out of breath again, running up the hill,

chasing my shadow across the stubble

to help the farmer unload his bales of hay.

NICK BOREHAM

IGLOOS

All morning the children have been outside

building igloos, ever since we awoke

to snow the length of the valley

as far as any of us could see.

The wind that shook the house last night

is less than a whisper now,

and they are outside, the children,

building igloos, cutting the snow into blocks.

The world they knew has disappeared:

farms and fields, barns and trees, roads and bridges,

all into a brilliant whiteness,

and they are outside, the children,

making it anew.

The sun has come out, the snow is beginning to melt

and our fear of the storm has gone.

Their mother appears

with scarves and steaming mugs of tea

and as they run to her, an icicle falls off the roof

and into a tub with a crack.

After all these years, I remember just as well

the birds' nest we found under the eaves that day

and the shouts of the children as they ran into the house

after their mother, laughing.

PANAYIOTIS VYRAS

ANGELS

Believe not what you see

But live it

Silence

A chorus sings

Even the turmoil in their praise

Goes upwards

Anchor

Your finest tone to sky

Be part of that assembly

Tear aside

All separating fogs!

PATRICIA SUMNER

EARLY MORNING, CILAN

Dew glistens the grey meadow. Light seeps
through cloud strata to silver the vale.
Treading the field in reverence, heads bowed,
silent heifers commence morning prayer.
Even swishing hooves are stifled
by the closeness of cloud, the stillness of air.

From somewhere, a rook scratches at sky –
its wings, snagged threads in silk –
till reluctant mist dissipates
and pine trees castellate the hill.

Now, like a tossed coin, night flips
and the vale is gilded with morning
and every tree bursts with blackbird and robin
singing the promise of dawn.

PATRICIA SUMNER

SYMPHONY

I shall inhale you.

I shall snatch you from the air
and breathe you in,
you shining minims, crotchets,
whirling semi-quavers.
And you'll tinkle like bells
through the hairs of my nose,
tingling, tingling.

Prestissimo violins,
you'll scurry down my throat,
flurry to fill
the great hall of my lungs,
where alveoli are choristers
and halleluiahs echo
under my ribcage dome.
You'll sing and sing.

From here, I shall absorb you.
Tumbling kettle drums,
you'll bubble-burst
into the thunder
of my blood,
where you'll gush to the rhythm
of my timpani heart,
pounding, pounding.

You will stir
my very core
with your frantic dancing.
You will orchestrate my song.
And the music I breathe
shall be joy.

PATRICIA SUMNER

MOMENT

(Tentsmuir, 18th August)
  for Jim and Lesley

Under a blue-sky festival,
a gazing woman sighs;
a dog, scattering swallows,
embraces the sand's meander;
a groom with a wide smile
feels the world beneath his feet;
a dew-eyed bride wonders.

And when evening ambers
the Dundee spires
and laughter steals
breath from our lungs,
electrons orbiting our every atom
know they are planets circling
this moment's sun.

RICHARD GILLS

SPRING

Golden sunlight stretches across the park,
ignites flowing grass – field of flames –
leisurely lapping in the tentative breeze.
I quicken my pace as sharp raindrops fall
from a clear sky, deepening all the colours
of the world, and stinging my bare hands.

The remnants of winter begin to decay:
frozen shadows recede and bright beads
trickle down and around the bony fingers
of branches. Memories of lifeless mornings
erode: the frozen stillness, without leaves,
without birds – when breath creates sculptures
 in iron air.

I strain to hear the distant flutter of wings
and watch the black V of returning birds,
outlined against the cotton clouds. Moving
along the path I touch the dark, damp soil –
where tight buds wait to be excavated by sunlight;
patient bulbs will explode into fireworks
of green stems, yellow and pink petals.

Trees and hedges twitch with anticipation,
preparing to swell with the volume of spring
and flex their sore biceps under leafy strain.
I watch a couple brandish a single umbrella,
defiantly, against the cleansing, jagged rain.
Serrated leaves will be here soon –
casting protective shade against forceful sun.

And as spring gently paws the tender earth,
stirring the stale dust of winter, waking hills
blossom into seamless green. The sky
offloads its grey overcoat and reveals
a pallet of blues, oranges, and red, reds.

SUSAN THOMPSON

WHO'S WITH ME?

Who's with me on this journey to short-lived eternity?
Who wants to take their time to get there, keen,
interested in all ideas, tell me more, absorbed, abstraction,
listen when the world's sore.

Have crazy thoughts, understand, see past short-sighted eyeline, command,
focus on distance to see the present, resistance is futile, indecent.

Lie down awhile, see the starlight, see tonight, see we are alright,
We're OK, abandon worry, console the lonely locked inside private minds,
send intuition, medicine, salve second sight for tears,
& never fear, I'm long in tooth, always strong & ever ready to coax reverie, disappear,
preferring others' timeless laughter to silent solo ever after.

NOTES ON CONTRIBUTORS

Arthur Carr

is a retired University Lecturer who began his career working as a volunteer in Tanzania, Kenya and Uganda. He spent further years working in the South Pacific Islands and nine years as a Training Officer in the Sultan of Oman's Armed Forces. Voluntary work in the UK included work with the Citizens Advice Bureau.
His interests include self-publishing books of poems, sailing; golf and playing piano. He has a wife Ann, (who edits the books of poems) and two sons – Stuart and Sean – and five grandchildren.

Bruno Alexandre Gomes Rodrigues

was born on the 31st October 1981 in Funchal, Madeira and was brought up in Portugal. He studied Forestry and Genetics before moving to England in 2011.

Claire Cox

completed an M.A. in Creative Writing at Oxford Brookes University in 2012. She has also given readings with her regular poetry group, *MsCellaneous,* and, with them, has published an anthology of group members' work.

Desmond Kon

is the founding editor of *Helming Squircle Line Press* and the author (under the name Desmond Kon Zhicheng-Mingdeé) of *I Didn't Know Mani Was A Conceptualist*, and *The Arbitrary Sign*, forthcoming in 2013. He has edited more than ten books and co-produced three audio books, several pro bono for non-profit organizations. He is the recipient of the PEN American Center Shorts Prize, Swale Life Poetry Prize, Cyclamens & Swords Poetry Prize, Stepping Stones Nigeria Poetry Prize, and Little Red Tree International Poetry Prize. An interdisciplinary artist, Desmond also works in clay, his ceramic works housed in museums in India, the Netherlands, the UK, and the US.

Don Nixon

has had a number of short stories publisahed (mainly in the crime genre) in anthologies and magazines in this country and North America. Wearing his other hat, he also writes poetry and has won various competitions including the formal award at the Italian Poetry on the Lake Festival in 2010 and 2011 and the Leeds Peace Poetry Festival in 2012. He has had work published by *Descant Magazine* in Canada. His first novel – *Ransom* (in the Western adventure genre) was published in January 2013. In the previous November he had two crime short stories published in the Crime Anthology – *Crime After Crime*. Both of these books are available in print and on download from Amazon. He is currently working on his second novel and a poetry anthology.

Dorrie Pearton

says that her poetry is mostly inspired by the countryside. She and her husband use their camper van to make an easy escape to the outdoors. There's always a notebook and pencil handy so little is missed. Sunshine means looking and rain means writing. The surprise is just how much there is to write about as every day presents something new. She shares her work with like-minded friends at a Barnet writing group.

George Reith

is a recent graduate from the University of Exeter, George has been published twice before as part of the *Secret Attic Collection*. He grew up in a variety of European countries, all the while writing poems, playing guitar and practising martial arts. George was also a media journalist for a number of years, but is now mostly unemployed.

Gwendoline Hartland

has been a member of a Creative Writing class in Enfield where she wrote poetry and short stories. From there, she joined the Enfield Writers' Workshop. She has written a mystery novel and a children's book

James Nuthall
is a charity worker with an MA in International Relations. He enjoys expressing his thoughts in rhyme to entertain friends and record what he feels passionate about. *We're in this Together* was the second poem he ever completed.

James O'Sullivan
James O'Sullivan is a native of Cork city, Ireland, where he is a PhD candidate at University College Cork. His work has been published in numerous journals and anthologies, in Ireland and beyond. He also dabbles in short fiction and photography. Further information on his work can be found at josullivan.org.

Jean Cardy
has had 3 collections published and many poems in magazines. She was a lecturer in English and now teaches 3 Creative Writing classes for U3A.

Judith Tremaine Drazin
is a widow. Her late husband was a Professor of mathematics at Bristol University. She is Cornish but has taught for many years in Bristol, and later worked in the hospital service. Writing has always been her great joy and relaxation; when her children were small, she wrote stories for *Listen With Mother.* If a story was accepted, it meant a new pair of shoes for one or other of the family.. Her daughter, who inherited her mathematical ability from her father, works for the National Audit Office. Her son is an anthropologist and is married to an anthropologist. She has lovely twin grandchildren.

June Drake
sport, not literature, was her main interest at school but her children drew her into it as they went through secondary school. She took A level literature as an adult student and enjoyed it so much that she did it again with a different syllabus. Now an octogenarian, she enjoys time reading and writing, especially poetry.

Luke Jackson

was born December 23rd 1991 in Banbury Oxfordshire. He emigrated to Austria at the age of 15 with his mother, step-father and younger sister, and began to write poetry there. The first poem he ever wrote was for his brother's wedding, which he read aloud to the hundreds of guests, and was titled *Love is*. He much prefers poetry with rhyming patterns and experimenting with them. He seems to produce his best work writing for, or about friends and family. His favourite poem is *A Runnable Stag* by John Davidson.

Margaret Pedley

has been writing for a few years now that she is retired. She writes mainly for herself - short stories and poetry and finds it therapeutic. She has been married for 30 years and has two grown up children. Lives in West Yorkshire and has a beautiful dog that she enjoys walking.

Mark Mikkelson

has been writing poetry with a serious passion since he was around 15 or 16 years old. His interests and the themes that his poems display, are diverse, but tend to have a noticeably individualistic angle. A few of his works have been published, most often by Forward Poetry. In April 2012, he was awarded first prize in the The Poetry Box International Horror & Dark Poetry Silver Cup Trophy Competition. Based in Cardiff, he is currently studying for his PhD in Psychology (Neuroimaging) at Cardiff University.

Meirion Tanner

is originally from Maidenhead in Berkshire, he has lived in London, Snowdonia, Bristol and Yorkshire and is now settling, slowly, in Manchester. His work has ranged from delivering groceries to leading expeditions in Africa and Russia, with some school teaching in between. Meirion began writing by accident and during a time of solitude and withdrawal whilst in addiction recovery. His writing speaks of a desire to find connection, strength, peace and hope in a world that can seem to be without these things.
He has published one book, *Dawnings* – see facebook.com/meiriontannerpoetry for more of his work and to contact him about his book.

Michael Borlase

Michael J Borlase was born in Plymouth, Devon in 1986 and has been writing poetry since his early teens. He writes conventional poetry, collaborates on multimedia works and performs spoken word poetry with musical accompaniment. He studied English at the University of Sussex and is a recent graduate of the London Metropolitan Creative Writing MA. His works deal with vulnerability, identity, art and loss. Michael currently resides in the city of Brighton.

Nick Boreham

lives in York. His poems have appeared in Aesthetica, Equinox, Poetry Scotland and A Thousand Cranes.
www.nickborehamauthor.com

Panayiotis Vyras

is a professional psychiatrist, born in Cyprus. Apart from medicine he has studied literature, traveled extensively and is fluent in many languages. Author of works on a variety of subjects (scientific, historical, psychological) in 2007 he started publishing poetry collections. Currently living in Athens, Greece: pano@vip.gr
Web-page for more inspirational poetry by same author:
http://www.amazon.com/Spiritual-Messages-Poetry-Panayiotis-Vyras/dp/1481812262

Patricia Sumner

was born and raised in North Wales. She now lives in the Vale of Clwyd with her husband and two children. She worked as a primary school teacher for ten years, specialising in English and Special Educational Needs. Now she works as a writer, editor and proofreader and runs her own business, 'Cilan Proofreading and Editing' (www.cilanproofs.co.uk).Her poetry has been short-listed in several national poetry competitions and has been published in poetry magazines and winners' anthologies, but this is her first poetry collection which won first prize in Thynks Publications' first poetry pamphlet competition. She writes children's stories for GoMadKids (www.GoMadKids.com), which are due to be published shortly. Her educational books on the teaching of creative writing are being published this year by Mr Educator Teaching and Learning Solutions (a division of GLMP Ltd). Her one-act play, *Help!* is available from New Theatre Publications, and her first full-length play, *Beyond Reach*, has been selected for a rehearsed reading at Chester's Little Theatre as part of their fifty-year celebrations.

Richard Gills

was born and raised in Gloucester, Richard's reluctant writing roots began when he studied for his Masters Degree in English Literature at Cardiff University. Some very brilliant lecturers mercilessly forced poetry upon him until he was forced to concede to a deep-seated fascination with the art. While poetry was initially a humorous and alternative outlet for Richard to express his day-to-day observations, this relationship steadily evolved into something more substantial and meaningful; as experienced in *Building Dams,* which was published in a collection in 2011. Several years later and Richard still relies on the cathartic power of poetry to provide a haven in which he can explore the nuanced avenues of his psyche, as well as the world around him. He also writes about his dog, Bess.

Susan Thompson

is an artist & poet who now lives in Malvern, Worcestershire with her daughter Lili.